The Creek and the Cherokee

D1716906

Kelly Rodgers

Consultants

Regina Holland, Ed.S., *Henry County Schools;*
Christina Noblet, Ed.S., *Paulding County School District;* **Jennifer Troyer,** *Paulding County Schools;* **David Proctor,** *Muscogee (Creek) Cultural Advisor;* **John Ross,** *Certified Cherokee Language Teacher;* **Karen Coody Cooper, M.A.,** *Cherokee Historian*

Publishing Credits

Rachelle Cracchiolo, M.S.Ed., *Publisher*
Conni Medina, M.A.Ed., *Managing Editor*
Emily R. Smith, M.A.Ed., *Series Developer*
Diana Kenney, M.A.Ed., NBCT, *Content Director*
Torrey Maloof, *Editor*
Courtney Patterson, *Multimedia Designer*

Image Credits: Cover LOC [LC-DIG-pga-07577], Wikimedia Commons, (background) Scott Barkley/ Flickr; pp.2 (top), 19 Lawrence Migdale / Science Source, (bottom) North Wind Picture Archives; p.3 (middle) ZUMA Press, Inc. / Alamy Stock Photo; p.5 (top) Corbis, (bottom) Granger, NYC; pp.j6-7 Courtesy of Gretchen Holcombe; p.8 Wikimedia Commons; p.9 Christian Heeb/ JAI/Corbis; p.12 George Catlin / Getty Images; pp. 3 (top), 13, 16-18, 26, 29; Marilyn Angel Wynn / Getty Images; p.15 Smithsonian National Museum of the American Indian; p.20 (right) Richard A. Cooke/Corbis, (left) Granger, NYC; p.21 (background) Kevin Fleming/Corbis, (top) Granger, NYC; p.22 North Wind Picture Archives; p.24 Granger, NYC; p.25 Corbis; p.26 (background) ZUMA Press, Inc. / Alamy Stock Photo; p.27 Buddy Mays/Corbis; p.29 Miguel Juarez Lugo/ZUMA Press/Corbis, (bottom) John Elk III / Alamy Stock Photo; pp.11,32 Town Creek Indian Mound State Historic Site; all other images iStock and/or Shutterstock.

Library of Congress Cataloging-in-Publication Data

Names: Rodgers, Kelly, author.
Title: The Creek and the Cherokee / Kelly Rodgers.
Description: Huntington Beach, CA : Teacher Created Materials, [2016] |
   Includes index. | Audience: Grades K to 3.?
Identifiers: LCCN 2015042454 | ISBN 9781493825530 (pbk.)
Subjects: LCSH: Creek Indians--Juvenile literature. | Cherokee
   Indians--Juvenile literature. | Indians of North America--Georgia--Juvenile literature.
Classification: LCC E99.C9 R65 2016 | DDC 975.004/97385--dc23
LC record available at http://lccn.loc.gov/2015042454

Teacher Created Materials

5301 Oceanus Drive
Huntington Beach, CA 92649-1030
http://www.tcmpub.com

ISBN 978-1-4938-2553-0

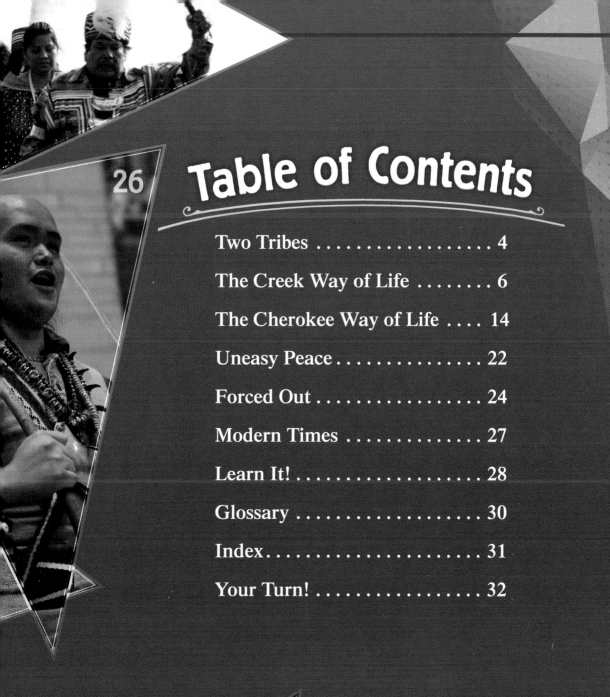

Table of Contents

Two Tribes

Long ago, Georgia was home to many American Indians. Some lived in the mountains. Others lived in the river valleys. They all lived in groups called **tribes**. In their tribes, people spoke the same language. They had the same beliefs.

There were two big tribes in Georgia. One was the Creek. The other was the Cherokee (CHER-uh-kee). These tribes do not live in Georgia anymore. But they left their mark on the state.

Mound Builders

The tribes in Georgia built complex cities. Some of their buildings sat on top of large mounds. A few of these mounds are still there. They are now museums where you can experience early American Indian culture.

Cherokee

Nacoochee Mound

Etowah Mound

Creek

Ocmulgee (ohk-MUHL-gee) National Monument

Kolomoki Mound

The Creek Way of Life

About 500 years ago, the Creek lived on land that would later be known as Georgia. The Creek were not just one tribe. They were a **union** of many tribes.

The Creek had their own way of life. They lived off the land. Creek men hunted and fished. They were also warriors. Some were even **chiefs**. Creek women farmed and cooked. They also took care of the children.

Creek

This is a model village at the Etowah Indian Mounds Historic Site.

Another Name

The Creek call themselves the Muscogee (muhs-KOH-gee) people. It means that they live on land that floods.

Food

The Creek women were in charge of the farming. They were also in charge of the cooking. They grew beans, corn, and squash. They made stews and corn bread.

Creek men used bows and arrows to hunt animals. They hunted deer and turkeys. They also fished in the rivers and creeks using spears and nets.

What Do the Colors Mean?

Creek warriors often painted their faces. Each color had a different meaning.
- Red was the color of war.
- White was the color of peace.
- Black was the color of life.
- Green was the color of night vision.
- Yellow was the color of death.

An American Indian hunter shows how to use a bow and arrow.

This is a re-created home at the Etowah Indian Mounds Historic Site in Georgia.

Home

The Creek lived in towns that had wooden fences around them. In each town there was a public square. People met there. There, they could do business and talk with one another.

There were homes where families lived around the public squares. The homes were rectangular. They were made of **clay daub.** They were also made of **river cane**. They had grass-thatched roofs.

This re-created village helps visitors learn about the Creek Indians.

Culture

The Creek have many dances. One is the Feather Dance. Boys who have shown they are ready are given war names. Then, the Feather Dance is performed.

They also have **ceremonies** (SER-uh-mow-neez). The Green Corn Ceremony is special. It is held when the Creek give thanks for a good **harvest**.

The Creek also tell stories. These **folktales** teach people about their culture.

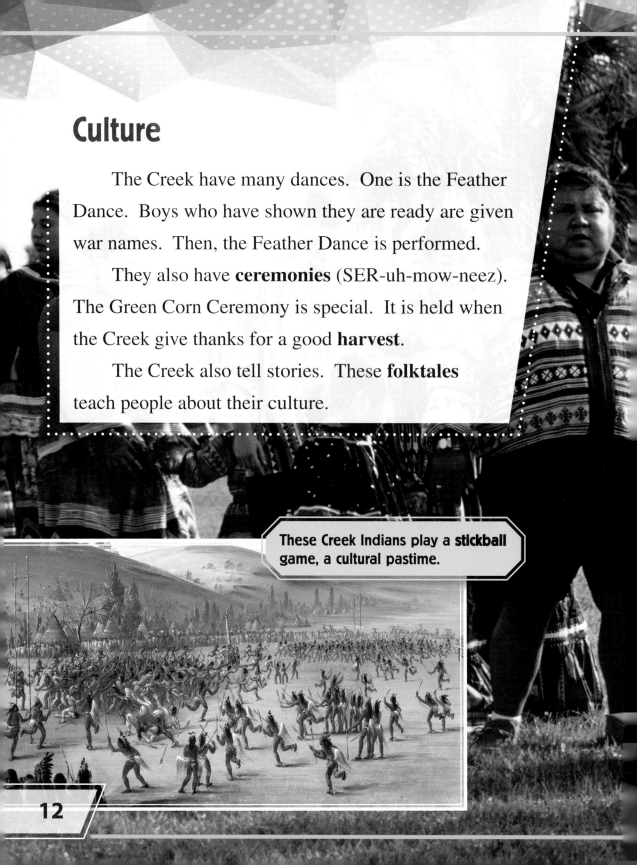

These Creek Indians play a **stickball** game, a cultural pastime.

The Stomp Dance is performed by many American Indian tribes at Green Corn Ceremonies.

The Cherokee Way of Life

The Cherokee lived in North Georgia. They lived in the Blue Ridge Mountains. They were a large tribe.

Cherokee people lived in villages. The men were hunters. They were also warriors. The women were farmers. They were also heads of their homes.

Cherokee

A Cherokee woman gathers corn in 1908.

Equal

Cherokee men and women had equal power in the tribe. Women were important in the family and had a voice in government (GUHV-uhrn-muhnt).

Food

The Cherokee men mainly hunted deer and turkeys. They only hunted for food. They did not hunt for sport. They also fished in rivers.

The women grew corn and beans. They also grew squash and pumpkins. Berries were gathered for food, too.

Three Sisters

The Cherokee and other tribes call beans, corn, and squash the Three Sisters because they help each other grow. Corn stalks let the beans climb. Squash leaves shade the ground. And beans make the soil fertile.

Home

The Cherokee lived in towns. These towns were often near rivers. Each town had about 50 homes. Families lived in their own homes.

They had two types of homes. Their winter homes were made of river cane and clay daub. Their summer homes were bigger and had more windows.

This re-created Cherokee winter house is called an *osi*.

This is a re-created Cherokee summer house.

Culture

The Cherokee had six main festivals each year. These were special celebrations (sel-uh-BRAY-shuhnz). There was a lot of food. And there were many dances.

One dance was the Booger Dance. Four or more men would dance in masks and costumes like "monsters." People mocked and defeated these monsters.

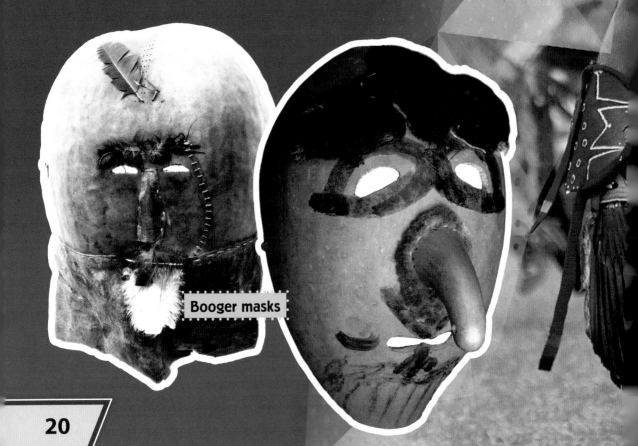

Booger masks

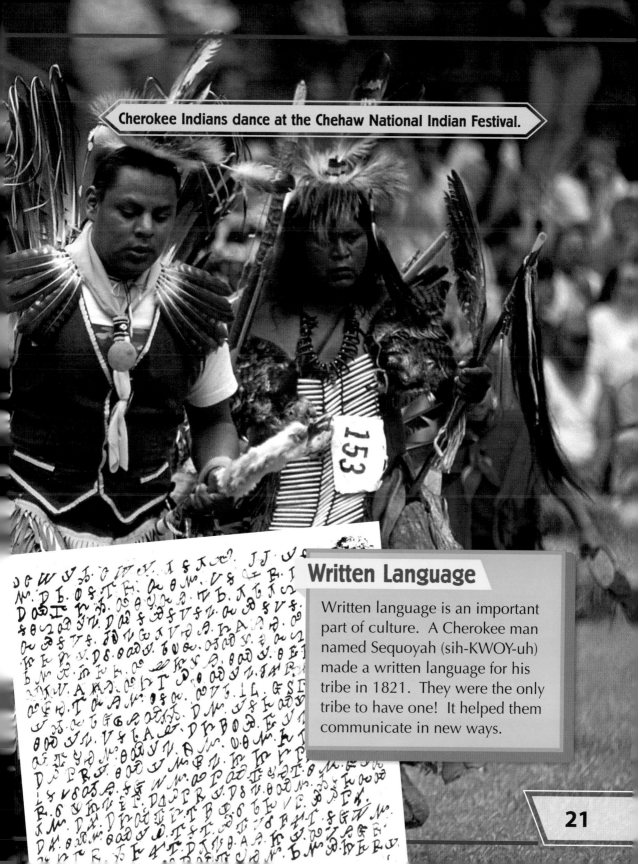

Cherokee Indians dance at the Chehaw National Indian Festival.

Written Language

Written language is an important part of culture. A Cherokee man named Sequoyah (sih-KWOY-uh) made a written language for his tribe in 1821. They were the only tribe to have one! It helped them communicate in new ways.

Uneasy Peace

Over time, more white **settlers** moved to places where the tribes lived. They took more and more land away from the Creek and the Cherokee. The tribes gave up many of their old ways. They hoped this would help them survive.

For a time, they were able to keep an uneasy peace. But it did not last. In 1830, the U.S. government passed a new law. All the tribes now had to move west.

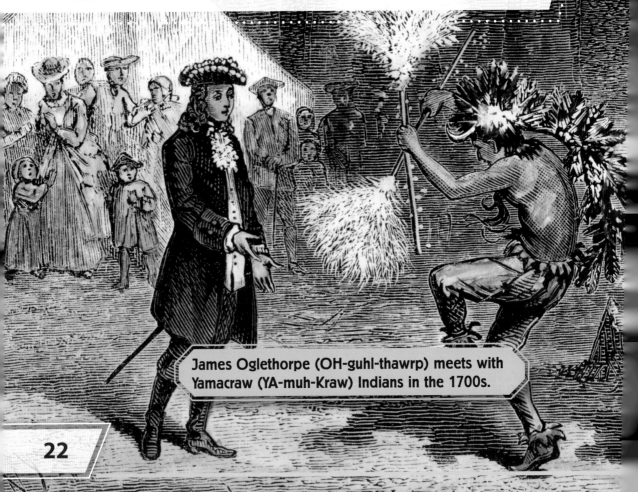

James Oglethorpe (OH-guhl-thawrp) meets with Yamacraw (YA-muh-Kraw) Indians in the 1700s.

Gold!

In 1829, people found gold in Georgia. This is one reason white settlers wanted to take American Indian land.

Cherokee

the Georgia Gold Belt

Creek

Forced Out

Some tribal members left Georgia after the law passed. But most Cherokee stayed. In 1838, the government sent troops. They forced the rest of the tribes out.

The tribes had to walk to Oklahoma. It was about 800 miles! It took months to walk that far. There was little shelter. There was little food. Many became sick and died. This experience came to be known as the *Trail of Tears*.

Moving West

Long ago, Oklahoma was called *Indian Territory*. The government sent many tribes there. This document tells which land was named *Indian Territory*.

Indian Territory.

Indian Territory has an area of 31,154 square miles, and by the census of 1900 had a population of 391,960. Indian Territory is an unorganized Territory of the United States, set apart as an Indian reservation in 1834. The section was a part of the Louisiana Purchase of 1803, with a western strip obtained from Texas. Its history begins with the advent in 1837, and since then only that of the nations — five nations and seven reservation — the nations having distinct Cherokees, Creeks, Seminoles, Choctaws — who own the entire a Governor and a Legislature subject to the indorsement of the Interior at Washington.

The land of the Territory is apportioned among the various tribes, each member receiving his share of ground. They are permitted to dispose of the land under certain restrictions. The Government has undertaken the listing of each tribe, and the work is partly complete. Each tribe has primary and academic schools for the children, supervised either by the Federal Government or the tribal heads. There are several railroads in the Territory, and each of these is rapidly increasing its trackage, so that many hitherto inaccessible sections may be reached.

Agriculture is the principal occupation in Indian Territory, although the increasing number of whites has brought about the development of certain manufacturing enterprises of local importance. Stock raising is carried on extensively.

By a Congressional act of May 19, 1902, munici-

ton. In the towns and on some of the farms are a number of whites who lease the ground from the Indians and live within the nations by special permit. Many have been adopted into the tribes and have tribal rights. The real Indian has not so much prominence as formerly, as there has been much intermarrying between whites and Indians and negroes and Indians. Many of the negroes now in the Territory are descendants of slaves formerly belonging to the Indians.

palities in Indian Territory with a population of 2,000 or more inhabitants were given power to issue bonds up to 10 per cent. of ther assessed valuation for the construction of public works, such as sewerage systems and water works, and for the erection of schools. Two-thirds majority of the municipal electors was made necessary for the issuance of these bonds and a sinking fund was to be created for the redemption of the bonds within twenty years. In these towns whose bonds had already been issued by

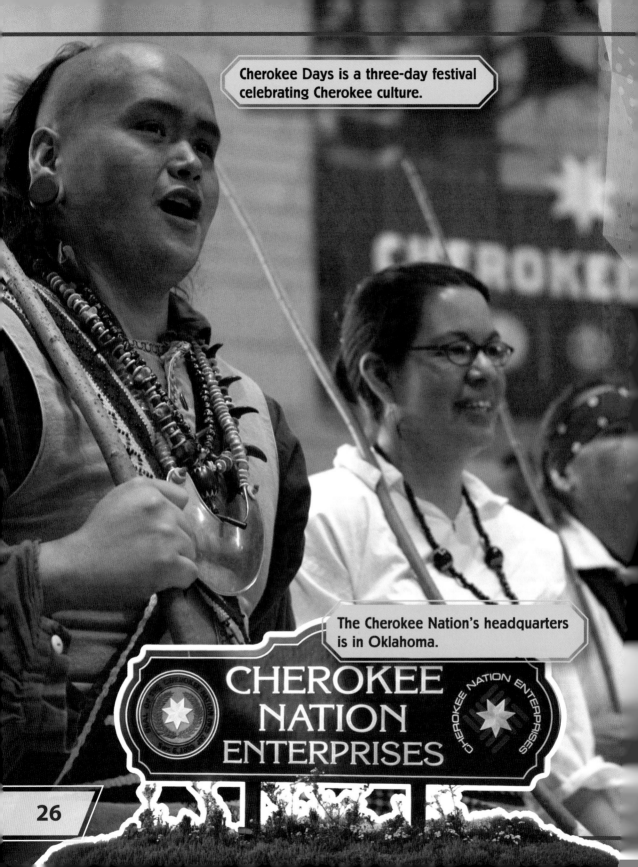

Cherokee Days is a three-day festival celebrating Cherokee culture.

The Cherokee Nation's headquarters is in Oklahoma.

CHEROKEE NATION ENTERPRISES

Modern Times

Today, tribal members live in different places. Many Creek and Cherokee are in Oklahoma. Many live in modern homes. They wear modern clothes. But they keep their culture alive.

Some still speak their own languages. They dance. They tell stories. They have a rich culture. And it is one they are happy to share with others.

Wilma Mankiller

In 1985, the Cherokee chose a woman to be their chief. They chose Wilma Mankiller. She was a great leader. She worked hard to improve Cherokee healthcare and education.

1828 – 1866

Learn It!

Long ago, there were many American Indian tribes that lived in Georgia. Find a third tribe that lived there. Read about the tribe. What food did the people eat? What were their homes like? What was special about their culture? Write your answers in a table like the one below.

I learned about the _____ tribe.

Food	Home	Culture

Glossary

celebrations—special events for an important occasion

ceremonies—events held because of a tradition or custom

chiefs—people who are the leaders of a group of people

clay daub—a sticky, heavy clay that is mixed with water and grass

festivals—special events where people celebrate

folktales—traditional stories

harvest—the amount of crops that are gathered

river cane—bamboo-like plant that grows in moist areas like swamps and river banks

settlers—people who go to live in a new place where there are few other people

stickball—a game similar to baseball that is played with a ball and a stick

tribes—groups of people that have the same language, customs, and beliefs

union—an organized group of people that have the same purpose and interest

Index

Your Home

The homes of the Creek and the Cherokee Indians look much different from homes of today. But some parts are the same. How is this home different from your home? How is it the same as your home? Draw a picture and label the similarities and differences.